Healthy Eating with MyPyramid

The Fruit Group

by Mari C. Schuh

Consulting Editor: Gail Saunders-Smith, PhD

Consultant: Barbara J. Rolls, PhD
Guthrie Chair in Nutrition
The Pennsylvania State University
University Park, Pennsylvania

Capstone
press

Mankato, Minnesota

Pebble Plus is published by Capstone Press,
151 Good Counsel Drive, P.O. Box 669, Mankato, Minnesota 56002.
www.capstonepress.com

1 2 3 4 5 6 11 10 09 08 07 06

Library of Congress Cataloging-in-Publication Data
Schuh, Mari C., 1975–
   The fruit group / by Mari C. Schuh.
   p. cm.—(Pebble plus. Healthy eating with MyPyramid)
   Summary: "Simple text and photographs present the fruit group, the foods in this group, and examples of
healthy eating choices"—Provided by publisher.
   Includes bibliographical references and index.
   ISBN-13: 978-0-7368-5370-5 (hardcover)
   ISBN-10: 0-7368-5370-7 (hardcover)
   1. Fruit—Juvenile literature. 2. Nutrition—Juvenile literature. I. Title. II. Series.
TX558.F7S38 2006
641.3'4—dc22   2005023716

Credits
Jennifer Bergstrom, designer; Kelly Garvin, photo researcher; Stacy Foster and Michelle Biedscheid,
   photo shoot coordinators

Photo Credits
Capstone Press/Karon Dubke, cover, 1, 3, 5, 9, 11, 13, 15, 16–17, 19, 21, 22 (all)
Corbis/Claude Woodruff, 6–7; Michael Prince, 5 (background)
U.S. Department of Agriculture, 8, 9 (inset)

The author dedicates this book to her friend Liz Odom of Fairmont, Minnesota.

**Information in this book supports the U.S. Department of Agriculture's MyPyramid for Kids
food guidance system found at http://www.MyPyramid.gov/kids. Food amounts listed in this
book are based on an 1,800-calorie food plan.**

**The U.S. Department of Agriculture (USDA) does not endorse any products, services,
or organizations.**

Note to Parents and Teachers

The Healthy Eating with MyPyramid set supports national science standards related to
nutrition and physical health. This book describes and illustrates the fruit group. The
images support early readers in understanding the text. The repetition of words and
phrases helps early readers learn new words. This book also introduces early readers to
subject-specific vocabulary words, which are defined in the Glossary section. Early
readers may need assistance to read some words and to use the Table of Contents,
Glossary, Read More, Internet Sites, and Index sections of the book.

Table of Contents

Fruit

Fruit helps keep you
healthy and strong.
What fruit have
you eaten today?

Do you ever wonder
where fruit comes from?
Fruit grows on trees,
bushes, and vines.

MyPyramid for Kids

MyPyramid teaches you
how much to eat
from each food group.
Fruit is a food group
in MyPyramid.

MyPyramid For Kids

Eat Right. Exercise. Have Fun.

To learn more about
healthy eating, go
to this web site:
www.MyPyramid.gov/kids
Ask an adult for help.

Kids should eat
about 1½ cups of fruit
every day.

Enjoying Fruit

Yellow, orange, red.

How many colors

can you eat?

Enjoy bananas, oranges,

and apples.

Pears, melons, grapefruit.
Fruit comes in
many shapes and sizes.
Try a fruit you've never
eaten before.

Strawberries make

a good snack

to share with a friend.

Sip, slurp, gulp.

Enjoy a cold fruit smoothie.

Smoothies have lots of fruit

in them.

Fruit makes a sweet part
of a healthy lunch.
What are your favorite fruits?

How Much to Eat

Kids need to eat about 1½ cups of fruit every day. To get 1½ cups, pick three of your favorite fruits below.

Pick three of your favorite fruits to enjoy today!

½ cup grapes

1 small orange

½ cup orange juice

6 watermelon balls

½ cup pineapple chunks

½ cup 100% fruit juice

1 small banana

½ of a medium grapefruit

½ cup + ½ cup + ½ cup = 1½ cups

Glossary

fruit—the fleshy, juicy part of a plant; fruit has seeds.

MyPyramid—a food plan that helps kids make healthy food choices and reminds kids to be active; MyPyramid was created by the U.S. Department of Agriculture.

smoothie—a thick, smooth drink made by mixing milk, low-fat yogurt, and fruit in a blender

snack—a small amount of food people eat when they are hungry between meals

Read More

Klingel, Cynthia Fitterer, and Robert B. Noyed. *Fruit.* Let´s Read About Food. Milwaukee: Weekly Reader Early Learning Library, 2002.

Nelson, Robin. *Fruits.* First Step Nonfiction. Minneapolis: Lerner, 2003.

Rondeau, Amanda. *Fruits Are Fun.* What Should I Eat? Edina, Minn.: Abdo, 2003.

Index

Word Count: 126
Grade: 1
Early-Intervention Level: 14

Internet Sites

FactHound offers a safe, fun way to find Internet sites related to this book. All of the sites on FactHound have been researched by our staff.

Here's how:

1. Visit *www.facthound.com*

2. Type in this special code **0736853707** for age-appropriate sites. Or enter a search word related to this book for a more general search.

3. Click on the **Fetch It** button.

FactHound will fetch the best sites for you!

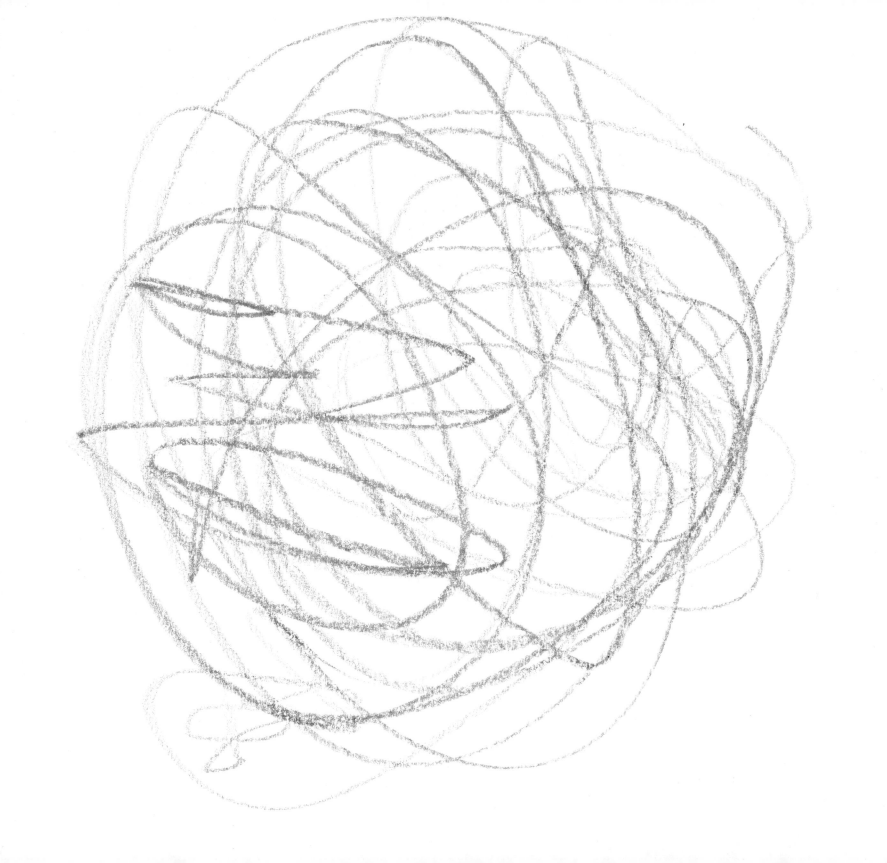